# ACCENT ON Christmas & Holiday ENSEMBLES

## Duets and trios for flexible instrumentation correlated with ACCENT ON ACHIEVEMENT, Book 1

**John O'Reilly and Mark Williams**

Dear Band Student:

Congratulations on becoming a member of the **band!** Another fun way to make music is to play in an **ensemble.** When you perform duets and trios with your friends, you become even more skilled as a musician. This book features Christmas and holiday ensembles correlated with specific pages in *Accent on Achievement*, Book 1, and is playable by students working in any first-year band method. You can play these ensembles with like instruments or with any combination of mixed instruments. Have fun making music together as you perform with *Accent on Christmas and Holiday Ensembles!*

*John O'Reilly*          *Mark Williams*

## TABLE OF CONTENTS

**Alfred**

# Jingle Bells

James Pierpont
(1822–1893)

# JOLLY OLD ST. NICHOLAS

Traditional

# UP ON THE HOUSETOP

Benjamin Hanby
(1833–1867)

# GOOD KING WENCESLAS

Traditional English Carol
(based on a Swedish Folk Song)

# AFRICAN NOEL

Liberian Folk Song

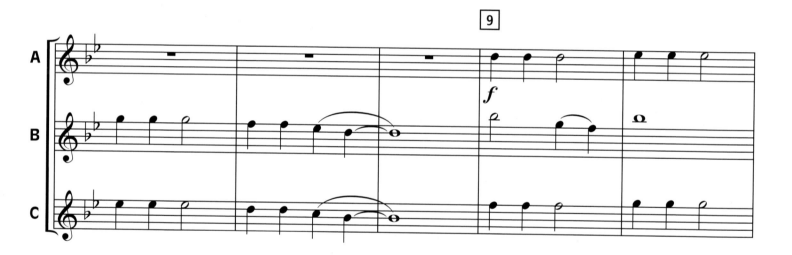

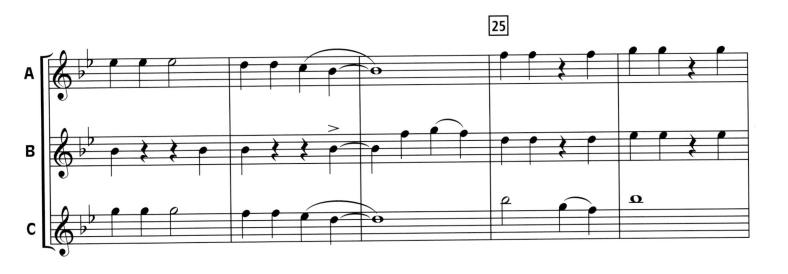

# HANUKKAH, HANUKKAH

Traditional

# Bring a Torch, Jeanette, Isabella

**Moderato**

French Carol

# DREYDL SONG

Traditional Hanukkah Song

# WE WISH YOU A MERRY CHRISTMAS

English Folk Song

# O Come, O Come Emmanuel

13th-Century Plainsong

# DECK THE HALLS

Traditional Welsh Carol

# JOY TO THE WORLD

George F. Handel
(1685–1759)

# Away in a Manger

James Murray
(1841–1905)

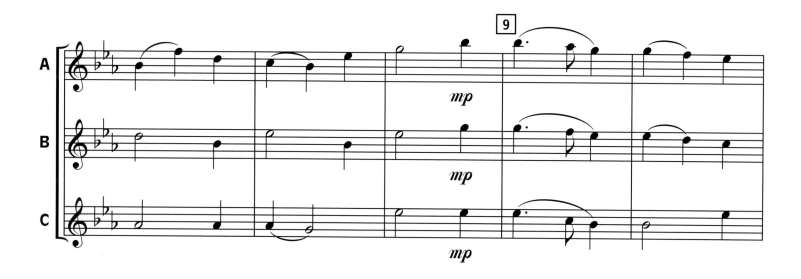

# WE THREE KINGS

John Hopkins
(1820–1891)

# THE FIRST NOEL

French-English Carol

# Angels from the Realms of Glory

Henry Smart
(1813–1879)

# HARK! THE HERALD ANGELS SING

Felix Mendelssohn
(1809–1847)

# ANGELS WE HAVE HEARD ON HIGH

French-English Carol

# Hanukkah, O Hanukkah

Traditional

# DING, DONG MERRILY ON HIGH

Thoinot Arbeau
(1520–1595)

# AULD LANG SYNE

Traditional Scottish Air

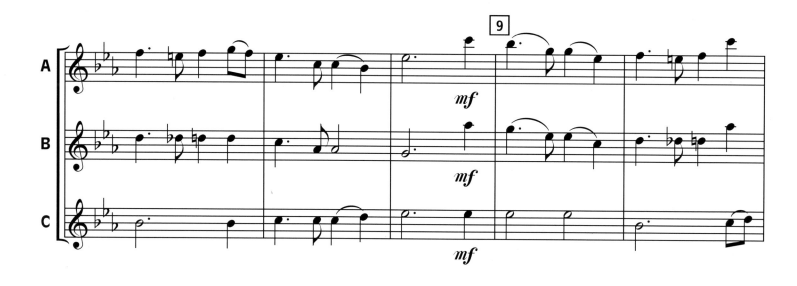